How to K   Purpose in Life

Why am I here?

What is my Destiny?

What is God's will for me?

Ask the question—then:

Watch for God's Answers!

God speaks to us in many ways.

Love Y'all,

Carolyn Barney

Carolyn Barney

This is a work of nonfiction.

Editing was completed Ann Blackbourn. Book prepared for publication by the Publishing Coordinator, Susan L. Harrington.

If you want to contact the author or if you'd like to contact the Publishing Coordinator, please Email: storiesforpublication@yahoo.com.

Printed in the United States of America.

BIBLE VERSE

"For I know the plans I have for you," declares the Lord. "Plans to prosper you and not to harm you to give you a future and a hope."

Jeremiah 29:11

WHO ARE YOU?

What is it about you that makes you unique and distinctly different from all other people? What is your make-up, personality, likes and dislikes, dreams, talents, and experiences?

> The Lord designed you exactly to His specifications to fit perfectly with what He is calling you to do with your life.

All of these contribute to who you are. You need to understand why you are the way you are before you can adequately discern your God-given purpose. The Lord designed you exactly to His specifications to fit perfectly with what He is calling you to do with your life. So, let's delve into why you are the way you are.

You do have a God-Given Purpose. The Lord will definitely answer when you pray, "Lord, what are You calling me to do? What is Your will for me? What is my purpose here?" God put that desire in you to ask because He has something special for you to do. He has a specific task, ministry, service, or good works waiting on you to fulfill. This is confirmed through the following scriptures:

Ephesians 2:10: "We are God's workmanship, created in Christ Jesus to do good works, which God prepared in advance for us to do."

Jeremiah 1:5: "… before you were born I set you apart, I appointed you…"

Jeremiah 29:11: "For I know the plans I have for you, declares the Lord, "plans to prosper you and not to harm you, plans to give you hope and a future."

Psalm 37:23: "The steps of the godly are directed by the Lord."

Proverbs 3:5-6: "Trust in the Lord with all your heart: do not depend on your own understanding. Seek His will in all you do, and He will direct your path." This is a promise from God to answer our prayers for direction. He wants us to know His purpose, and the Lord guides each step along the exact path He has laid out specifically for us.

We want to know His will, but the problem is sometimes we don't realize or catch the Lord's guidance. God is actively speaking to us about our every move, but we are missing it. He is answering our prayers for guidance, but we don't hear or catch His answers.

Romans 12:2: "You will know what God wants you to do." Per this promise, God will make His purpose perfectly clear to you.

You do have a God-given purpose!

The Lord caused this book to be written to help you understand and recognize some of the many ways God communicates with us. His directions usually are not given through His audible voice. So how does the Creator of the universe speak to us? We ask the Lord for direction, but we fail to catch His answers because we do not understand God uses many different ways to instruct us.

The Lord's methods can even include Miracles, in which He makes the impossible happen, and Divine Appointments in which He makes sure you are in the right place at the right time to receive His message usually through other people. But, you must connect the experience with His answers or you will miss it!

That is the key to this book. You will learn how to connect the dots, put two and two together, note the patterns, and reflect on all the parts that comprise the whole picture of the puzzle.

This book is in two parts. The first part is to help you know yourself in order to ascertain your calling in life. To this end, I have given some ideas for thought as to why you are the way you are. The second part is to help you understand some of the many ways God speaks to us.

For this purpose, I have given you my personal experiences as practical examples of the various ways the Lord has used in guiding me into several different ministries and His perfect will for me.

First, in understanding what God is calling you to do; you must realize that He has specifically designed you to fit the exact purpose He has prepared for you. God has already given you all the abilities, talents, and skills and desires you will need for this assignment. It is according to His plans that the Lord created you exactly like you are. Even your personality and your experiences will fit perfectly into your mission. You were custom made by the Creator to fulfill His work, and so you are like you are for a reason--His reason. Thus, you can use your specific characteristics, personality, temperament, and design as clues to help you determine your assignment and purpose in life.

The following topics will help you pinpoint what you were created for. Consider your own personal desires, dreams, interests, likes and even your dislikes. These will help you discern your purpose.

> Consider your own personal desires, dreams, interests, likes and even your dislikes.

What do you love to do? What do you care about the most? What do you get passionate about? What are you really good at? What do other people say you are good at?

The answers to these questions serve as guidance to where God wants you to serve. In general, people do great at what they love to do but don't usually succeed at tasks they don't enjoy doing. Consider your own abilities and talents that God has placed within you. These abilities can be used in ministry by serving the Lord through helping others.

What are your favorite activities, sports, and the hobbies that you love doing? If you love to care for little babies, then the Lord may ask you to work fulltime in a Church nursery. But, the reverse is also true because if you can't sing or carry a tune, God may not call you to be main soloist in a concert choir.

What do you like to do? What can you do really well? These are strong indicators of what God wants you to do. Whatever it is that you are good at and love to do is probably what the Lord is calling you to do. Don't be afraid that God will call you to do something you definitely don't want to do. If the Lord is asking you to do it, He will give you the desire to do it, however, if you know what the Lord is asking you to do, but you are resistant to do it, the Lord has ways of encouraging you.

Psalms 37:4: "Delight yourself in the Lord and He will give you the desires of your heart." Consider your desires, what is it you would like to do that will help and serve others?

One Preacher's son did not want to preach until after his father died. Then, all of a sudden he wanted to preach and he became a successful Preacher. To this day he loves to preach and would not choose any other occupation.

You should also pay attention to your personality and character. Some of us are introverts, and some are extroverts. Some always want to be around crowds and some don't. Some people work well in a team while others work best alone. God designed you with the right personality for what He is asking you to do. Realize that your character will fit your purpose.

Your spiritual gifts can also help you discover God's will in what He is calling you to do. Many Churches offer courses and literature that can help determine your personal spiritual gifts and give suggestions on where and how to use them. The gifts that God has placed within you can direct you towards areas of service.

Some of these gifts include the following:

a. Teaching: This gift gives you the ability to explain things in a way all will understand. You enjoy sharing what you have learned with others. You may also have the ability to write well.

b. Organization: You are goal and task oriented. You have great organizational skills and have the ability to coordinate things to get the job done.

c. Service: You love to serve and help others, and also enjoy joining groups that are volunteering and serving.

d. Mercy: You are especially sensitive to the hurting of others and have compassion for those suffering. You want to help those in distress.

e. Encouragement: You desire to encourage others and give much needed words of comfort. You are willing to share your personal testimonies to help motivate and lift people's spirits.

f. Hospitality: You love to welcome guests into your home and seek opportunities to do so. You want people to come to your home for their meetings and events.

g. Giving: You usually have the desire and resources to give to others, charities, and ministries. You look for reasons to give, and it brings you much joy to do so.

h. Evangelism: You have a strong desire to share the Gospel with non-believers and will gladly go where you are needed.

i. Preaching: Preachers are shepherds of their flock, their Church. You have the responsibility for your congregation's long-term spiritual growth.

j. Leadership: You have the ability to lead others and to motivate others to accomplish their tasks and goals. In addition, God uses your experiences to mold you into what He is calling you to do.

Additionally, besides the spiritual gifts, consider your educational qualifications. What jobs did you enjoy doing most? What did you do on your vocation that you could use to help others?

For me, I had to keep a journal on the job and using these journal notes, I had to write large reports. From this, I developed the ability to take large amounts of data and compile them into specific documents. I used this same skill to help others by writing this book created from the notes I made in my many Prayer Journals throughout the years. I also learned how to use a computer in writing reports which I also used in writing this book. What skills did your work teach you that you could use to help others and thereby serve God?

God also uses our painful experiences. Your test becomes your testimony and your mess becomes your message to help others going through the same thing. Your personally will then be uniquely qualified to share with hurting people how the Lord comforted you, loved you, and brought you through your crises. This will in turn bring them comfort, and give them hope and encouragement to also turn to God and rely on Him for their support during their difficult, trying time.

Make a list of what you are good at and love to do.

In summary, the scripture says in Ephesians 5:17: "Don't act thoughtlessly, but try to understand what the Lord wants you to do." Think about it. Pray about it.

Assess your skills and abilities, likes and dislikes, and your experiences. Assess who you are as to your personality and temperament. Make a list of what you are good at and love to do. What you really loved to do in the past may be what the Lord has for you to do in the future or some variation of it.

Consider your whole picture of who God designed you to be. Look at all the individual puzzle pieces of who you are, and then see how they fit together as a whole. Each piece fits perfectly with what the Lord is calling you to do. And remember, you will have a desire to do it!

It is a win-win when God wants us to do something and we want to do it. We are far more likely to go for it if we have a desire to do so.

God is working things out behind the scenes.

Some of you have been seeking God's calling and specific will for your life for some time. When it seems no progress is being made and you are waiting on the Lord to open doors, you can easily become frustrated and discouraged to the point of giving up.

But be absolutely assured of this, God is working things out behind the scenes. God's timing is always perfect, so don't jump ahead of Him. The Lord wants you to fulfill what He has called you to do--your purpose and your destiny. Don't get discouraged. Be patient with God. Renew your hope.

Your specific calling will happen--but in the Lord's timing. We have to trust Him when things seem like they will never happen. Don't give up!

Remember, we see only part of the picture, whereas the Lord sees the complete finished picture.

> Pray and ask God for wisdom concerning your purpose and just start reading God's Word.

The question is how does the Lord communicate with us so we can specifically discern His purpose for our lives? The best way to know God's will for you is to go to God's Word, the Bible. This is His Instruction Book that will help and guide us in all things.

First, pray and ask God for wisdom concerning your purpose and just start reading God's Word. If no particular chapter or verse comes to mind, then just open the Bible and start reading.

Does a Bible story seem to fit your particular circumstances? Does a certain verse or passage of scripture seem to catch your attention? For me it was 2nd

Corinthians 9:8 which states, "And God will generously provide all you need. Then you will always have everything you need and plenty left over to share with others."

With this verse as guidance, I joined a Church's Ministry giving out clothes to people and started a Baby Basket Ministry for newborns.

Also, what do you hear from other Christians about some service or ministry they are involved in? Are you also interested in that ministry? If you hear from several people, over a period of time, that you ought to be a Preacher, then at least consider it. Have you always wanted to go on a Mission trip? Do you love to travel?

The Bible says it is important to note it when there are two or more witnesses. Remember, if the Lord is calling you to be a Preacher, don't dismiss it because right now you don't have any desire to preach. When the time is right and if this is your calling, you will desire it, can't wait to do it, and will absolutely love doing it.

We also hear from God through sermons and books, especially devotionals. Many times the Lord has used these in my life as guidance and confirmations. I listen to a lot of preaching. Whenever a sermon is talking about what I am currently experiencing or is teaching me something new, I write about it in my Prayer Journal along with the date. This, too, can be a way to hear from God, so I strongly encourage you to start one today.

> The Lord may put or allow unusual events in your life to get your attention because He has something to say to you.

I often reread the journals and see if there is a pattern of the same things being said by different people in a short period of time. Many times the Lord does use my Prayer Journal entries to guide me and help me see the whole picture.

Also, don't dismiss circumstances. The Lord may put or allow unusual events in your life to get your attention because He has something to say to you. One recent event occurred two days after I asked God if He wanted me to do a video concerning artwork for a ministry.

In this circumstance, I heard two people talking out back of my home and looked out the window. Just at that exact moment, one of the two guys had a video camera pointed exactly at my face. They were about to take down trees in the back and were filming the area as to what was in the way of any falling limbs or trees. This had never happened before and at first startled me which made me pay attention to it.

Later I did the video; however, this was only one of several confirmations to do so. (I like to get several answers from God concerning His guidance about something. Some confirmations have more weight than others.)

Another time I was seeking God's will concerning buying a new special camera for taking high-quality pictures needed in a ministry I was doing. Just after I asked the Lord about it, I was at Church and a special event was taking place. A lady was standing in the aisle taking pictures with her fancy camera directly beside me as I was sitting on the end seat.

Yes, this is a small insignificant piece of the puzzle, but I also had other confirmations that I, indeed, was supposed to buy this camera. A great answer happened when I told my family to give me money for Christmas because I wanted to buy this special equipment. I did not tell them the price, but the Lord was probably smiling and saying "yes, get the camera" when the family without knowing it, gave me the exact amount of money that the camera cost.

Pay attention to all the various ways the Lord answers your prayers and the timing of them. After you ask the Lord a question, look for immediate answers within a few days. In other words, if the lady taking pictures had been two weeks later, it would not be as significant a confirmation as if it took place soon after the question. I give a lot of weight to what happens next after I am seeking guidance about something from God.

Finally, you will have a complete peace regarding the assignment of God. Again, when you want to do something, you generally will have a peace about it. If everything is perfect except for one little thing that keeps bothering you, pay attention to it. Seek additional guidance from the Lord. It could be that this is what the Lord is calling you to do, but it may not be His exact perfect timing or your understanding is not exactly correct yet. The Lord will make His will and your purpose and timing completely clear to you.

PRAY & WATCH

After you have made a self-assessment of whom the Lord has created you to be, you should have a better understanding of who you really are. The next step is to simply pray and ask the Lord as to what He is calling you to do. Then, watch for God's answers! This is the fun part because His answers can be astonishing and amazing!

> Then, watch for God's answers!

Some of the ways God communicates or speaks with you are listed below:

1. Read through various scriptures and Bible stories.

2. Pay attention to what other Christians are saying to you.

3. Think about what you are sensing in sermons and books.

4. Note what thoughts come to mind while you are praying; give God time to speak to you.

5. Discern the true meaning of your circumstances.

6. Consider any patterns in your experiences.

7. Watch for God's confirmations.

8. Assess if there is complete peace regarding the assignment of God; not partial peace.

The rest of the book contains real life examples of hearing from God through answered prayers and confirmations. It is especially important to realize that circumstances are great indicators of His guidance for you to do or not to do something.

> Circumstances are great indicators of His guidance for you to do or not to do something.

The following chapters are examples of my real life experiences on how I heard from God while applying these eight activities listed above plus others.

For many years I have asked the Lord questions and recorded His direct answers and indirect confirmations in my Prayer Journals. My personal experiences will give insight and understanding into many of the ways the Lord communicates with us. But remember, God is not limited to just the ways I have written about.

I WAS TO WRITE A BOOK

One of the ways God speaks to us is through <u>Christian books and literature</u>. One day I was reviewing and rereading the recent entries of what I had written in one Prayer Journal. I noticed comments from a devotional which asked that after praying, "Do you have confidence that God will answer? Are your prayers specific enough that when God replies, do you notice the answer?" It continued to suggest that you write down your particular request, then, pray specifically for this petition and watch for God's answers.

> Are your prayers specific enough that when God replies, do you notice the answer?

It had been on my mind about writing a book from my Prayer Journals, which are my spiritual autobiography. I chose to request guidance as my petition. I then prayed for answers about writing a Christian book concerning the contents of my Prayer Journals.

Just after this prayer, I received immediate guidance as I continued to read my Prayer Journal entries. This stated to consider long-range projects such as, to "write a book". Another entry said to take time today to write out a testimony of your spiritual pilgrimage. It added that others will be encouraged upon reading your spiritual autobiography.

The Lord continued to give me guidance about writing this book through noticing patterns of things occurring over and over. Another journal entry said: "For the next week, focus your prayers on your request." So, I decided to seek God by rereading all the entries I had written in my Prayer Journal over the next week. I received the following answers for His guidance which actually occurred on the same day of that week:

1. Jeremiah 30:2: God said to Jeremiah, Write down for the record, everything I have said to you."

2. Jeremiah 36:2: "Get a scroll and write down all my messages... Begin with the first message...

and write down every message <u>you have been given, right up to the present time</u>."

3. Jeremiah 36:18: "...I <u>write down His words with ink on this scroll</u>."

From the answers the Lord gave me, I understood I was to write this book, and it was to be about the things I had written in my Prayer Journal. These included my testimonies, Christian experiences, and my questions to the Lord and His answers. But, I also love to get additional answers or <u>confirmations</u>, from the Lord regarding my understanding of His will for me.

I asked the Lord if I had correctly ascertained that this was His will, to have a Preacher, next Sunday, say the words, "Prayer Journal." Two days later, on Sunday, a Preacher on television that I usually watch said the words, "Prayer Journal". This was a direct answer to a prayer for discerning God's specific purpose for me. Thus, I concluded that my guidance was to write a book about all the occurrences the Lord had impressed on me to write down in my many journals.

God also speaks to us through <u>Sermons</u>. I was rereading, in my Prayer Journal, a sermon which said that Paul at the height of his career was thrown into prison. This allowed Paul to <u>write letters to the Churches which later became books</u> that now appear in the New Testament.

The Holy Spirit used this statement from this sermon to catch my attention and prompted me to pray, "Do you want me to still write a book about the experiences in my journals?"

The Lord speaks to us through <u>Christian people</u>. Just two days later after this question, I received the answers to God's will for me. I was listening to a lady on TV who said that <u>she shares her testimonies in her new book</u>. Also, later that day I heard another lady say: "<u>You are going to be writing and telling me what God has done</u>."

Another way to hear from God is through <u>what other people say to you</u>. One Saturday, while on the way to Pigeon Forge with my Sunday School class, I told the person next to me about some of the experiences I had recorded in my journals. She asked me if <u>I was a writer</u>, and having never written a book before I answered, "No". She said <u>I should "write a book" of all the experiences I had recorded in my Prayer Journals</u>.

Then just after that, the very best answer for guidance occurred while watching a third lady on TV. She made the statements, "<u>You need to write a book and start writing that book</u>!"

Finally, I had a total <u>peace</u> about writing my first book, because I knew it was God's will and calling for me to do so. I had this peace because I had received the Lord's many answers and confirmations so I had no doubt, whatsoever, that this was my purpose.

HOW GOD SPEAKS TO US

Many years ago I took a Church Bible Study Course. This Bible Study was designed to teach us the ways God speaks to us. Its purpose was to assist us in knowing what God's purpose and plans were for our life. This study

> Hearing God through prayer, Bible scriptures, preaching, Christian people, circumstances, and peace.

taught practical ways in which to hear from the Lord and mentioned hearing from God through prayer, Bible scriptures, preaching, Christian people, circumstances, and peace.

James 1:5 says "If you need wisdom--if you want to know what God wants you to do--ask him, and He will gladly tell you." This is a promise from the Lord to us. So, when you are seeking His direction and answers, the first thing to do is to pray and specifically ask Him for wisdom and understanding.

Then, go to your Bible and turn to a passage that comes to mind and you are led to. You can read an entire book, chapter, page, or a few scriptures and keep on reading until you understand what God is conveying to you. The Lord will take a passage and make His will evident to you. Remember, God will always confirm His answers.

> God will always confirm His answers.

I was working through the Church's Bible Study Course and completing everything the text was asking me to do each week. The study related that the Holy Spirit would quicken our insight as to what the Lord was telling us through whatever Bible text or story He gave us. So, I read several different passages in the Bible and noticed a pattern that a lot of the verses dealt with "prisons". I was instantly aware of how unusual that was, because the Holy Spirit was quickening me to note every occurrence.

It was a very long time ago, so I do not remember if this study course taught you to ask for confirmations. But, I was learning, and so I tried it anyway. I asked God if this was indeed His intent for me to notice "prisons", and to give me other Bible verses as confirmations that spoke of prisons. And the Lord did--three consecutive times.

Encouraged by this, I asked the Lord to give me Acts, Chapter 16 where Paul and Silas were praying at midnight in "prison" when their chains fell off. Then I opened my Bible one time, and it went directly to Acts, Chapter 16. We definitely can't limit God as to the innumerable ways in which He speaks to us. I knew these were not coincidences. God was speaking to me through these activities of a possible Prison Ministry.

The course also explained that God also speaks to us through what people say to us. While I was taking this course study, a lady came to my office, which was very unusual because we don't get visitors. During our meeting, she happened to mention that she had just returned from a Bible Class at the clubhouse of her retirement home.

We spoke a minute about the course that I was taking, and in her conversation she mentioned she was personally interested in doing "Prison Ministry"! Through her conversation, I quickly understood this was a <u>Divine Appointment</u>. God sent her to help me realize that in people's conversation there can be a word from the Lord tailored just for me.

I was starting to see a theme; I saw the pattern of God bringing up the word, "prison", to me. I then prayed that the Lord would give me a confirmation regarding the Prison Ministry by having a Christian person, my Sunday School teacher say the word, "prison".

The next day, when the teacher started the class, she interrupted her normal study by saying that there was just something on her heart that she had to share with us. She began to tear up as she related that last night, she was watching the show, "Larry King Live", and was so touched with what happened that she just had to tell us about it.

She said that during this show, Billy Graham was the guest and when another well-known man came out, Dr. Graham went over and hugged him even though this other man had just gotten out of "prison". (This showed that he fully accepted him.)

> God does speak to us through prayer, Bible scriptures, and other people that He sends to us.

Why did a Sunday School teacher mention the word, "prison"? Because God arranged it! It was another <u>Divine Appointment</u> set up by God to answer my prayer. God used her to speak to me regarding His will and to show another way in which He speaks to us. The Lord wants us to know His will and not have any doubt about it. His Word, which is the Bible, promises the Lord will make it clear.

Now I began to understand as I went through each week that God does speak to us through prayer, Bible scriptures, and other people that He sends to us. I also found God will confirm His will.

It is so exciting to know the God of this whole universe communicates personally to us. And as the Lord does it for me, He will also do so for you because the Bible says He is no respecter of persons. This means the Lord does not favor me over you.

All you have to do is to watch for His answers and be aware of the ways the Lord uses to answer our petitions. That is the key--recognizing his answers so you can know God's purpose for your life. Before this study course, I think the good Lord had been answering my requests, especially for guidance, but I just was not catching them.

> When you catch God's answers through circumstances, it can be the most exciting way of hearing from God because it can be incredible.

I also learned through the study that another way God speaks to us is through circumstances. When you catch God's answers through circumstances, it can be the most exciting way of hearing from God because it can be incredible.

One circumstance occurred when the Lord showed me a new insight regarding the seven Churches listed in the Book of Revelation. I prayed that God would send me a Christian Jew. (I felt that I needed to speak with someone who had both a Jewish and Christian perspective concerning this new God-given insight into the Churches.) Soon I realized this was the Holy Spirit prompting me to specifically pray for this.

Two days later, I was in a book store. In the middle of the aisle, there was a man sitting at a table with books on it. As I passed, he asked me if I had accepted Jesus as my Savior, and I said "yes". He asked again, and through this question he caught my attention, and so I stopped to talk with him.

I explained that when I was younger, I realized I was a sinner. So I had asked Jesus to forgive my sins because I believed Jesus had specifically died for my sins and had risen from the grave. I told him that I totally believed that Jesus is the Son of God. I explained that I had indeed asked Jesus into my heart and had accepted Him as the Lord of my life and Savior of my soul--that I know He is real.

One way I personally know and have evidenced that God is real is by the answers He gives to my prayers--just like those for guidance as explained in this book.

If you are not hearing from God, are you sure you have accepted Jesus as your Savior? This is the first step and the most important thing you will ever do in this life.

What are you hearing when you seek God? Is it messages about salvation or messages about what service the Lord is calling you to do? Pay attention. Discern His voice. God speaks for a reason.

After my brief conversation with this man at the table, I was about to move on. However, the lights went out in the store so I lingered at his table for a few minutes as the registers were closed and I could not check out with my book. This was not coincidence, because I then noticed the book on his table had a Menorah on it. I asked him if he was Jewish. He answered that he was not only Jewish but also a Christian believer. In fact, he was a Preacher— a Christian Jew! At that moment, I recognized this was a

<u>Divine Appointment</u> and a direct answer to my direct prayer.

I immediately asked him if he was interested in the Churches listed in the book of Revelation in the Bible. He said "yes", and I asked if I could meet with him and explain my insight concerning the seven Churches. He told me to come by next week, and I did.

I explained to him my understanding of these messages for over an hour. He politely listened intently to all I said never interrupting. After I finally stopped and asked him what he thought, his answer was very surprising! He said, "interesting". That's all--just "interesting"! Somehow, that was definitely not enough. I knew God meant for me to talk to him, but I was not getting any feedback--nothing at all.

Then I understood why I was there because just after his one comment, he apologized for having been late. (It seemed he was late because he had been conducting a "prison ministry" which lasted longer than usual. There it was, Prison Ministry again. I caught it.)

I instantly understood why this circumstance of wanting to speak to a Christian Jew had occurred and why God had deliberately put him literally in my path. It was truly a Divine Appointment. Also, it explained why at the bookstore, the Lord had me stay and talk to him by causing the lights to go out at the exact moment I was at his table. Now you can understand why it was definitely not a coincidence!

This taught me that on the surface circumstances can seem to be for one purpose, i.e., insight into the Churches, but underneath look for what God is really saying to you. By noticing the patterns through prayer, the Bible, Divine Appointments, preaching, and circumstances, God was teaching us to discern His will.

There was one last activity to do in this course. Once we had determined what we thought God was saying to us, and we believed we knew God's will for our calling, we were then to state this purpose back to God in prayer. I learned that after we pray, we were to get up off our knees and pay particular attention to what happens next.

Late one night, since I believed God was calling me into this ministry, I did exactly what the course said to do. I prayed, related back to God my understanding of my purpose, and then watched and waited for what happened next.

First thing next morning I went to work. As I was opening the door to the office, I saw a friend who worked in the office next to mine. As I had already told him of the experiences I had been having in this course, he knew about this possible ministry. He approached me and stated, "Hey Carolyn, have you been out to the prisons yet?" (Wow!)

I shared all of this with my Church Bible Study Class who was taking the course with me. Now I wondered which ministry? I knew of several including Mike Barber, Kairos, and Chuck Colson Prison Fellowship. But before I could start trying to figure out which one, God provided the answer.

One of the ladies in the Bible Study happened to know that this Church had the Chuck Colson Prison Fellowship

Ministry already established, and was looking for volunteers. She furnished the name of the man in charge and his phone number. (There is no such thing as coincidence.)

> He does communicate with us if we will only pay attention and catch the many ways He does speak to us.

Sure enough, that was exactly the ministry God was calling me into. Before I had even finished the course for discerning God's will, I knew what ministry, exactly which ministry, and the contact person. God is good! He does communicate with us if we will only pay attention and catch the many ways He does speak to us. I obeyed God's calling, and the ministry became the love of my life for years to come.

GOD'S PROTECTION

God was calling me into an Evangelistic Men's Prison Ministry. But I am a female, a Southern Belle, who has never been in trouble with the law. Therefore, I was nervous about going into that environment not knowing what this would be like and if it would be safe. The Lord took care of all my concerns over my safety. He did this in quite a unique way.

The experiences God used to once and for all alleviate any of these fears included allowing me to go through a series of wrecks, accidents, and near accidents--all within six weeks! God's ways are interesting to say the least. Proverbs 3:5 states that "His ways are not our ways."

God started getting my attention when an impossible car accident occurred. I say impossible because I was in a company car driving down a totally deserted highway in Mississippi on a perfectly sunny clear day. My car was the only one on the road when a car on a side street ran a stop sign and hit the side of my car.

I distinctly remember a voice, an Angel perhaps, telling me not to put my foot on the brakes as I was trying to regain control and keep my car on the road. I was, however, wildly veering back and forth across the two-lane highway. If any car had been coming, it would have been a head-on collision. But God kept me safe without even a broken finger nail and also kept the driver in the other car totally unhurt.

Second, I was in someone else's van in New Orleans while going to lunch, when a fellow co-worker backing out of the restaurant parking lot, hit our van. The place where the car hit was right at my door. Again no one in either car was hurt at all.

Then, a week or two later, I was driving on a two-lane road. The roads were wet and a large trash truck coming towards me lost control and slid on the wet pavement crossing over into my lane. We were now driving straight toward each other in the same lane and it would be a head-on collision. However, the Lord kept us from injury and from crashing, as I was able at the last second to turn off the road into a parking lot. Fortunately, the trash truck stayed straight and slid right past my car. We missed each other. Thank you Lord!

Shortly after this, I was in Mississippi, with work, when a tornado hit close by where I was staying in a room on the top floor of a hotel. I heard the hard pounding rain and saw the way the wind was bending the trees and causing a lot of flying debris. I ran and cowered in the bathroom for a few minutes until I heard a fire engine's siren from a long distance away coming closer and closer to my position. Then I heard another and another, and ambulances and police cars all coming one at a time with sirens blaring. They seemed to stop right at my hotel.

I was too curious to stay put any longer. I hesitantly went to the large plate windows, which thankfully did not break, and peered out through the still blinding rain. I saw all of these emergency vehicles composed in a circle surrounding both sides of the road beside my hotel.

On closer scrutiny, I noticed that my hotel was fine and had come through the tornado without incidence. However, the hotel across the street had lost its roof which was lying across the road. The road was being secured by the emergency crews. The local news channel the next morning announced that it was the only tornado that had occurred in Mississippi that day—and I had been in the middle of it!

Also during these six interesting weeks of near disasters and wrecks, I also slipped in the bathtub, taking the shower curtain down with me. Again, I was completely fine but could not remember ever in my life falling in the tub before.

The sixth incident occurred when I was again driving in Mississippi. I was driving in some hills, and had the nervous feeling that I did not want the flatbed truck driving close behind me to stay behind me. I was very much aware that I needed to pull off the road and let the truck pass, but there simply was no safe place to pull over. I was driving through the boonies with frequent turns and going up and down hills.

Finally, even though it was not a designated pull-over area, I saw a little extra space on the side of the road, jammed on my breaks, and scooted over as far as I could to let the truck pass. No sooner had I done so, and then at the next curve around a hill, I came across the truck which had slammed into the car ahead of it. Once again, God had saved me from harm.

The lesson I learned was this: God uses circumstances, even negative strange ones, to get our attention. Allowing unusual circumstances to "happen to us" is the Lord's "attention getter". He has a purpose for whatever you are experiencing. Through circumstances, the Lord is prompting you to seek Him and ask why you are going through those particular events in your life. The reason is that God has something special to say to you, and if you are not already paying attention then, He has to get your attention--or in my case, alleviate my fears.

> God uses circumstances, even negative strange ones, to get our attention.

Not immediately catching the reason I was going through these events, I prayed and asked God why these unique, but quite scary things, were happening to me. The Lord then answered and gave me His perspective on why I went through all of these incidents, one right after another, in such a short time.

Remember, we hear from God through <u>Christian literature and Bible stories</u>. So after praying, I read my morning devotional, and through it the Lord totally answered my question. The devotional was about the story of David and Goliath in the Bible. The Holy Spirit quickened my understanding. "Carolyn, do you see that David knew God would <u>protect</u> him from Goliath because God had already protected David from the bear on one occasion and from a lion on another occasion. Therefore, David knew God would protect him from the giant before him. And He did."

At this time, I already knew that God was calling me into Chuck Colson's Prison Fellowship Ministry. The Holy Spirit revealed to me, through this story that the Lord was going to protect me from harm during this ministry. He had just protected me through wrecks, near wrecks, a tornado, and falling, all without being hurt. God was showing me He had been right there with me protecting me the whole time I was going through these scary situations. Thus, I now knew that God would protect me while I was doing His work in the prisons. I was not to be afraid. Fear was not going not to stop me from obeying the Lord in joining this ministry.

> If everything seems perfect except one little thing does not seem quite right and is bothering you--then don't do it.

The deciding way to know that we have heard correctly as to what God is calling us to do is having a peace about doing it. If everything seems perfect except one little thing does not seem quite right and is bothering you--then don't do it. It is either not God's timing and you need to wait, or you have misunderstood some part of the calling. However, don't let fear stop you. 2nd Timothy 1:7 states: "For God has not given us a spirit of fear and timidity..."

Realizing this, I had <u>perfect peace</u> and was never afraid for one moment during the years I was a part of this ministry. Like David, who God had promised would be King, God had given me His <u>Personal Word</u> that He would keep me safe--and He did. (Thank you, Lord!)

PRAYING FOR A JOB

Psalm 37:23 states, "The steps of the godly are directed by the Lord." This example is given to help us understand that our steps are ordered by the Lord even though we may not recognize it at the time.

Many years ago, I had a job with a university. The Lord gave this position to me through a Divine Appointment with the Chancellor who was a member of the Restaurant Club where I was a hostess. One day, out of the blue, he said he wished I had a Bachelor's Degree because the university had a recruiter job opening. To his surprise, I informed him I did have this degree. I had an interview with his staff and was hired. I loved the job, and it fit me perfectly.

About two years later, I wanted to move to Atlanta, Georgia. I needed a job and could not afford to be without one. I took my vacation, and with resume in hand, went to Atlanta to visit my brother and sister-in-law and to look for a job there. I arrived Saturday, and Sunday the newspaper stated there was to be a large Job Fair that week at Atlanta's Convention Center.

Of course I went to the Job Fair. As the Lord had planned it, I had all the necessary qualifications to meet many of the job offerings. I submitted my resume for several different positions. While there, one man in particular encouraged me to apply for a particular position that was not listed and I did. A few months later, this same job opened up, and I was offered the positon and took this God-given job. I loved it and stayed with it until retirement.

Another way the Lord speaks to us is by <u>reviewing all of our circumstances, experiences, and events that happen while we are seeking His will.</u> This is done by looking back on what has happened and lining up the events in order to see the whole picture of all that we are experiencing. In this circumstance, I saw from beginning to end that this new job was "God-ordained".

Per His plans, God was ready for me to move. He put the desire in me to move to Atlanta. Then at <u>exactly</u> the right week, I had to take a job hunting trip <u>specifically</u> to Atlanta which had this particular Job Fair <u>only</u> for that week. (There had not been this type of major Job Fair in Atlanta for many years before, or since, this one.)

Through God's ordained circumstances, I was in <u>the right place at exactly the right time</u>. The Lord had provided me with a place to stay (my brother's family) while I looked for a job. He provided me the exact person, another <u>Divine Appointment</u>, to ask me to apply for a position which I did not know about. It was this job the Lord had waiting for me. What an awesome God we serve. He promises to guide the steps of His children, and He does answer prayer!

JESUS SAYS "I LOVE YOU!"

A few years ago, I was in one of those seasons in which I was not hearing anything from the Lord. It was like there was a great gulf fixed between us, and I could not feel His presence or His love for me. I missed our communications dearly and wanted to know if He was still with me.

During this "desert time", I had to take a road trip for my job over to Alabama from Louisiana. On the drive there, I decided to give that drive time to God through singing hymns, praising him, praying, and most importantly-- telling the Lord just how much I loved Him. If I could not hear from Him, then at least I could show the Lord my love for Him.

And I did--all the way there. I enjoyed doing this so much that I had to remind myself to keep my hands on the wheel because I kept on raising my arms to the Lord while singing songs of worship.

Proverbs 16:9 states, "In his heart, a man plans his course, but the Lord determines his steps". Again, pay attention to circumstances--especially patterns. After I finished my work in Alabama, I began my drive back home. Just as I left Meridian, Mississippi, I "accidentally" took a turn off from I-20 towards New Orleans--not towards home.

I say "accidentally" as I was in the turn-off lane before I realized it. The traffic which had been moderate at that point was so dense I could not get over into another lane. I had to take this wrong road. The Holy Spirit then prompted me to sense that things happen for a reason and God was up to something! I distinctly remember asking the Lord, "What are you up to?" I turned around and drove back to I-20.

I drove on to Pearl, Mississippi, stopped for a cup of coffee and to stretch a minute. As I drove into the parking lot, I saw a parked car with a hand-written white cardboard sign stuck in the back window that said in large letters, "JESUS LOVES YOU". Other than noting it at that time, I did not think too much about it.

Later during the drive, I came up behind an 18-wheeler that had printing on the back which said, "JESUS LOVES YOU". As I drove closer to home, I came across a moving van that printing on the back of it, "JESUS LOVES YOU AND IS COMING BACK SOON."

Finally, as I arrived back home I drove past a billboard from a local Church at one of the intersections which showed a picture of Christ in white robes with His arms outstretched with the caption, "JESUS LOVES YOU".

Wow! Does God know how to make a point or what! The Lord, in His own special way, let me know He did love me! This revealed that God was hearing my prayers, and He was with me all the time and had been with me all the time--even when I did not feel the Lord was there. But He was there, and He had never stopped loving me and will never stop loving me. The scriptures say that the Lord promises to never leave us nor forsake us. This means He is still there even when we do not sense His presence or hear from Him.

God has a purpose for what He does and for what you are going through. I believe with all my heart that the purpose for His long silence was to include this circumstance in this book to encourage you. It was so that you too would know that at those lonely times in life when the Lord seems far away and your prayers are not answered, Jesus is still with you, and does in fact loves you!

WAIT ON THE LORD

One of the ways we hear from God is by <u>putting the</u> <u>experiences we are going through together with the timing</u> <u>of their occurrences</u>.

Many years ago I was living in an apartment and decided I needed to move. Though it was a wonderful apartment, after a while it got a little small for my needs. Also, I had been there several years and I strongly desired a home. I asked the good Lord, more than once, about moving. I soon realized waiting on the Lord is hard--very hard. We live in a microwave world, "Lord I need it now please".

> Waiting on the Lord is hard.

After the last time I prayed about moving, I heard a sermon which said that sometimes God wants you to "stay put" right where you are. He added, "Not to be discouraged but to wait accepting that God knows what is best for you and is in control."

Because the Holy Spirit had quickened me to note the "stay put" part of this sermon, I felt prompted to ask the

Lord if He wanted me to "stay put" and not move to a home at that time. In order for me to definitely know His will in this matter, I prayed that the Lord would give me the Bible story of Isaac who was told by God during a famine to "stay put" where he was. Isaac was to plant crops there during the draught, and not to move to Egypt.

The day after I had prayed, I was reading a devotional. It said that as you read your Bible and pray, listen to what God has to say to you about His will for your life. The Holy Spirit prompted me to immediately turn in the Bible to the reading for that day.

My Bible is divided into daily readings so one can read through the entire Bible in one year. So that day's reading was Genesis, Chapter 26 which was the Story of Isaac! Coincidence? Never! In verses two and three, God told Isaac, "Do not go to Egypt. Do as I say and "stay here" in this land. If you do, I will be with you and bless you." I believed the Lord was expressly telling me to "stay put" and not to move at that time.

God also speaks to us through social media especially if the timing is perfect. As I am writing this "stay put" testimony for the book, the very minute I had finished it, I decided to read my email and there it was--an email from the staff at my apartment complex to me personally which stated that they hoped I was not thinking about moving. It continued that sometimes the right decision is to "stay" exactly where you are and keep your current address. And it added at the end that they were hoping to hear that I would "stay put" and not move. What a <u>confirmation</u>! Our Heavenly Father just loves to find neat ways to bring a smile to our faces.

> Our Heavenly Father just loves to find neat ways to bring a smile to our faces.

BLESSING IN DISGUISE

We can also seek God's will for <u>specific things and needs as well as for our purpose in life</u>. Sometimes what we ask God for comes through a circumstance that I call a "<u>Blessing in Disguise</u>".

> We can also seek God's will for specific things and needs as well as for our purpose in life.

I stayed in the apartment a few years, but every so often I would check out the housing market with my realtor cousin. We would drive around and see if there was anything out there that would be suitable. I would ask God if it was now His will for me to have my own home. At the time, it seemed God's will for me was not to become a home owner.

I was praying for very specific things regarding my dream home. I asked God for a one-story, end-unit townhome that would have a wood-burning fireplace and be in a good, safe neighborhood. It should also have privacy from the bedroom windows, plenty of trees, fenced, and have two bedrooms. I further requested of God that the house would fit comfortably within my price range with a very low interest rate.

In December, my cousin and I were again driving around the city looking at houses, especially in the neighborhoods I was most interested in. I was very discouraged because once again I did not find any home that fit my criteria. It still seemed that was not God's will for me to move at that time.

At the end of our search, I pointed to a cute little cobblestone town home with a stone chimney and remarked to my cousin, "Why couldn't God give me a home like that one with the magnolia tree in the front yard." It, however, was not for sale.

In January, I was conducting my job at a facility that had been having problems. At the beginning of the job, I left paperwork for the Manager that contained our corporate address.

One person at the firm pointed to the New Orleans address and said it was good that only the New Orleans address was listed and not the address of the local office where I worked. He then explained that in case someone wanted to send a bomb to our agency, it would only go to the New Orleans address. He looked me in the eyes and stated, "I know where you live." And he did too! He revealed to me exactly which apartment I lived in.

I became instantly nervous. I quickly finished my work at the firm and left. I instantly reported the incidence to my Supervisor, who said, "Write a memo". I did and it got lost. It all appeared to be forgotten. Or so it seemed, and I calmed down too.

Two months later in March (God's timing), the Director of my agency in New Orleans found the memo. To say the least, my world turned upside down quickly. "What do you mean we have had a bomb scare? Carolyn, go the FBI, go to the police now, today!"

Forget calm - I got frantic! Immediately that day, I went to the FBI and contacted the police. The FBI told me, "Mam, if I were you, I'd <u>move</u> right away since he knows where you live." The police woman said the very same thing and also strongly advised me to <u>move</u>--immediately!

I instantly called my cousin and told her that I had to find a house, and asked if she could meet me after work. She said she could, and we sailed off looking for homes. I remember thinking, at this time, that I could not wait on God any longer because time was an issue. Today was the day, and whatever homes were available were contenders. We drove around visiting several houses in my price range. However, none of them, not one of them, was suitable.

To say the least, I was highly discouraged. About 8:30 to 9:00 p.m. that same night, my cousin went home to check her listings to see if there was anything she might have missed or that had just become available. Not wanting to give up, I continued the search in the dark, driving in just those neighborhoods I wanted to live in.

As I was leaving the last neighborhood, I noticed a house with an open front door and lights on. There was no For

Sale sign, but I could see there was no furniture in the house, and a man was inside painting the walls. I pulled over, knocked on the door, and asked if he was getting the house ready to sell. He said that he was, but there were already a couple of buyers ahead of me who were interested in the house.

I asked if it was okay for me to come in and look around, and he invited me in. Please understand, it is night, I am alone, and I am entering the house of a total stranger. Under other circumstances, I probably would not have so boldly gone in. But this was different because there was urgency.

I walked through the house all of two minutes, looked out the back door, and began to cry in front of this perfect stranger. In answer to his strange look at me, I responded by asking him if he believed in the power of prayer. To my surprise he said, "Well yes, I am a Deacon in my Church, and I believe in prayer." I told him that I had prayed for a town home, end unit, with a fire place, two bedrooms, with privacy, and trees, just like this one.

His answer was God ordained. He said to me that if I felt God was giving me this house, then he would not stand in God's way and if I qualified, the house was mine. I had been so excited that I had not even asked the price until after he said this, and yes, it was comfortably within my price range. And I qualified. It "just so happened" that the interest rates at that time were at an all-time low!

God was at work and directing my steps all along. God had not said "no"; it was just a matter of His perfect timing! The next day when it was daylight, and I was less excitable, I noticed the front of the house. There it was -- the magnolia tree, the cobblestone front, and the stone chimney.

> God had not said "no"; it was just a matter of His perfect timing!

In fact, it was "the house" that, when all discouraged, I had pointed to earlier with my cousin asking aloud why God could not give me a little house like that one. God, with a smile on His face, gave me the very home that the Holy Spirit had prompted me to notice and point to. Of all the homes in this area, God gave me that one.

Coincidence? No! It was God's blessing, but it came at first in disguise as a very fearful circumstance.

Geneses 50:20 states, "You intended it to harm me, but God intended it for good to accomplish what is now being done..." The Lord took what was meant for my harm, the bomb scare, and turned it into my good--answered prayer for my home. God is listening even when we don't see any results right away. It took two years, but in God's timing, He gave me everything I had prayed for in a home and more.

Even when circumstances seem negative on the surface, God is still in control working behind the scenes. God used this scary event to propel me to go house hunting the very day He had this blessing waiting for me. The Lord set up the Divine Appointment between the home owner and me. He caused both of us to be at the right place, at the right time, and with the right heart. It was the will of God for me to own that specific home. I just had to wait for God's perfect timing. Be encouraged!

ANSWERED PRAYER— FINALLY!

There is <u>no</u> such thing as coincidence; it is God's guidance! Pay attention to <u>coincidences</u> especially those where you think, "What are the odds of this happening?" Pay attention to God's timing.

> Pay attention to your circumstances after you pray!

I love the Blue Ridge Mountain area and took rock-hunting vacations there with my family. While in Franklin, North Carolina, I prayed and asked God to let me know if He wanted me to move to North Carolina, which was the heart of rock-hunting country. Two days later, my sister and I were sluicing, which is washing dirt off rocks, at the one of the ruby mines in Franklin. Only about eight people were present.

A lady sat down beside me and said she was from Shreveport, Louisiana (Me too.) and she was born at Schumpert Hospital. (Me too.) She mentioned she was moving to North Carolina and wanted to buy a ruby mine, but the deal fell through that morning. Lastly, she said that her name was Carolyn (Me too!). What are the odds? That is when you know "it's a God thing". Remember, God's answers can be astounding!

Pay attention to your circumstances after you pray! Exactly two days after my prayer, God gave me a "know-that-I know" answer through that stranger sitting beside me named Carolyn, who was born at Schumpert in Shreveport, and was planning to move to North Carolina! The odds of all of these "coincidences" happening together at the same time would be astronomical; especially just two days after seeking if it was God's will for me to move to there. The Bible says that we meet Angels unawares. "Was she one?" Later, I wondered.

This was definitely God's answer to my prayer for guidance. No other answers or confirmations were needed.

Since I now knew it was God's will for me to move to North Carolina, I wanted to go immediately, but also knew I had to wait for His timing. I asked the Lord when He was ready for me to move from my cobblestone home, have someone out of the blue, come to my door and make a cash offering to pay Fair Market Value on my house. Then I would know it was His timing.

In the meantime, over the next two years, I found several snakes in my yard. One day, I had a snake in the folds of my garage door that bit me (Non-poisonous – thank you, Lord) when I was cleaning the door. Let me say, I really, really don't like snakes, and this was just about more than I could stand!

Almost exactly a year later from the garage door snake incident--the "last straw" happened! (I found then and there that God also works through "last straws".) There was again a very live four-foot snake in the folds of my garage door. He was trying to come down on top of my head just as I was about to get groceries from the trunk of my car which was under the opened garage door overhead.

Needless to say, I cried out loudly for God to help me, and He immediately caused the community maintenance man, Divine Appointment, to be at the end of my driveway as I screamed. (God's perfect timing!) He came running over and we both killed the snake. Yes, there was no way on God's green earth this snake was getting away to slither back into this garage again. This was the last straw for my staying in this house. I just could not take another snake, and what if one got into the house?

After I recovered from this scare, I remember telling God, "I'm sorry, but I can't wait on you any longer because this was just one snake too many." I explained to the Lord that I felt I had to sell this house right away and get out now! I felt I could no longer patiently wait for God to make a way--not realizing of course, God was using all of this, and my sense of urgency, to accomplish His will.

Due to my zeal to get out quickly, I immediately started discarding from my house anything and everything I was not willing to move. I had been at this home, which I loved, for many years and had a lot of "stuff" that I did not want to take with me. In God's provision and guidance, there was to be a community-wide garage sale that weekend after the snake incidence. I had a lot of stuff that was out in the garage for the sale, as well as lots of throw-away junk loaded in large yard sacks at the front curb.

And the garage door happened to be open. A man, seeing all this stuff outside, walked up to my house came through the open garage door and asked me if I was getting ready to sell the house. It should be noted, that at this time, there was no For-Sale sign on my property and no realtor was involved. I immediately said, "yes", and he promptly offered to buy my house at a Fair Market Price and pay cash!

Romans 8:28 states, "We know that God causes everything to work together for the good of those who love God and are called according to His purpose for them." After the initial shock, it finally dawned on me God was answering my prayer exactly the way I had asked Him to when it was His time for me to move to North Carolina.

I would never have dreamed that God would use a snake, much less cause it to work together for my good. I am not saying God caused the snake to be there, but He allowed it for His purposes. I just had not immediately equated the snake as part of God's plan (Who would?), but it clearly was.

In Jeremiah 29:11, God says, "I know the plans I have for you - they are for good and not for harm, to give you a future and a hope." Looking back over all these circumstances, I realized what was meant to harm me (the snake) was used by God for my good (my calling) which was His plan for me to move to North Carolina.

The snake had directly influenced all the sacked junk to be out by the curb. Then God's Divine Appointment caused the buyer to be in the neighborhood at that exact time in order to see the accumulated trash sacks out front and subsequently to offer cash for my home. God's timing! God's perfect timing! I sold the house and a week later was in North Carolina looking for a place to live.

THE LORD HONORED MY REQUEST

God also speaks to us through <u>reassurance</u>, if you will ask Him for it. Often assurances come through listening to <u>preaching</u>.

I prayed and asked the Lord if He would honor His name, "The Great and Awesome God" because I was asking the Lord for a Miracle that only He can do.

Just two days later, the Lord honored His name by answering another prayer in a wonderful, precious, miraculous way. When I moved to North Carolina, per the Lord's call, I left my Mom who was fairly healthy and doing okay for someone 94 years old. She was in a safe nursing home. My sister and brother-in-law were also there, in the same town, to help take care of her.

I asked the Lord specifically that even though I was following His will to move to North Carolina, I would like to be able to say good bye to my Mom when the Lord chose to call her home. I thought I would have a few days' notice, before she died, so I could be with her and tell her I loved her. God is so faithful.

It did not happen like I thought it would, but it was definitely a blessing. I woke up dreaming about my Mom, and to my remembrance, I had never dreamed about her before. In the dream, she came walking in the front door of my home while I was deciding where to move my furniture. She visited a while, and I walked her back to her apartment, not her Nursing Home, and my sister met us there. As I was waking up, I told her I loved her.

Mom died six days later. I believe God sent her to me so we could say goodbye to each other. I was also able to be physically with her before she died, but because she was in a coma, I was not able to communicate with her. God worked it out another way through the dream.

This dream was God's way of answering my prayer and honoring His name, "The Great and Awesome God." Thank you so much, Lord!

THE LORD WILL GIVE REASSURANCE

As I knew my Mom was sick a few days before she died, and knowing this was probably her time to go, I was feeling guilty that I had left home a few months earlier and now Mom was dying. I asked the Lord for reassurance that I did right in coming to North Carolina. Was it truly His will for me to do so? Had I made a mistake?

The Lord's answer came the same day from a sermon I heard. The Preacher referenced Matthew 14:21-22 and said that after performing the Miracle of feeding 5,000 people with five loaves and two fish, Jesus told the disciples to get into the boat and cross to the other side.

They were there according to His specific instructions. But then, a storm came, and they had to struggle to stay afloat. Then, Jesus performed a Miracle and calmed the waves saving all the disciples. The Pastor remarked that Jesus put the men there, and you, too, are where the Lord put you.

He finished the story by relating that Jesus knew the men were in the path of the storm, and you are exactly where God wants you to be. The Minister then asked us to say the out loud that God has me where I am for His purposes. Then, he added that this is a Word of the Lord for somebody tonight. (Yes, me!)

NO PEACE IS ALSO GOD'S GUIDANCE

Another ministry which the Lord has called me into is helping people, especially with food and clothing needs. In my home town I had volunteered through a Church fulfilling this type of service and loved it! When I got to North Carolina, I began volunteering through a Community Service Program that also offered food and clothing. Immediately, I was offered a small job with them. As I was volunteering, I was learning the position to determine if I would be a good fit for the possible position.

> The Holy Spirit will send you a red flag of uncertainty, doubt, or the feeling that this is not right for you when God wants you to <u>not</u> do something or to stop.

But soon an incidence occurred that left me with no <u>peace</u> about taking this community job. Through this experience, I learned that the Holy Spirit will send you a red flag of uncertainty, doubt, or the feeling that this is not right for you when God wants you to <u>not</u> do something or to stop. Likewise, the Lord will send you a green light of ease, peace, and love for it when He is saying, "Yes, do it." Simply put, I had no peace at all about taking this position.

I prayed and asked the Lord what was His will regarding my taking this job? I was asking this because they did give out food and clothing, which I was called to do, but they did not let you freely talk about Jesus there. This bothered me. When things bother or disturb you, ask the Lord why.

> When things bother or disturb you, ask the Lord why.

God answers through <u>Christian people and sermons</u>. Two days later, the Lord gave me the answer through a sermon. I heard his sermon taken from II Kings 7:3-9. For the past few years this Bible story regarding the four lepers at the Samaritan wall was my personal Word from the Lord concerning giving food and clothing. I have heard this story many times.

In this story, the town of Samaria was starving because the enemy had them surrounded for a long time. There were four lepers that, due to the starvation, left the wall where they stayed and bravely went to the enemy's camp hoping they would give them some food and let them live.

As they were approaching the enemy's camp, God performed a miracle and magnified their footsteps so that the enemy fled in fright leaving behind all of their supplies, which also included food, clothing, and water. Then the four Lepers ate and had their fill. The Lord also put it in their hearts to return to Samaria to tell everyone about all the food and supplies so that the whole town was saved.

The Pastor's sermon, however, added a new dimension to that Bible story that I had never heard before. Basically, he said that "Yes, we as Christians need to feed and clothe people and to help meet their physical needs. But, even if we could give every person three meals a day and all the clothing they want, there is still the issue of their spiritual needs. We have the responsibility to seek out those who need what we have spiritually."

God told the Churches to go boldly and share the Gospel of Jesus Christ with our neighbors. The Pastor also related that you, too, need to share your story of God's love to those who need to hear it. They need to hear it, and we need to tell it. It is interesting to note that the Pastor said he waited until now to give this sermon due to recent circumstances in his life. This is not a coincidence; it is God's perfect timing!

Through this sermon story, I understood the Lord to say to me that it was more important to share the Gospel of Jesus Christ than it was to just serve alone. This was a direct answer to a direct prayer. I knew beyond a shadow of a doubt that God was telling me to not take that community job.

God's Word says that the Lord has a plan for us, and He wants to accomplish something great through us. God never leaves us to figure it out by ourselves if we will seek His will. God promises Christians that He is going to guide us in whatever He calls us to do and will make that very clear to us. God did this for me--He will do it for you. Watch for His answers.

When we can't see the direction we should take, God will take the time to assure us that we are walking directly in the path He wants us to walk in. Likewise, the Lord will also let us know when He does not want us to do something. All we have to do is ask Him and again, we must understand how to recognize His voice. The more God answers prayers and directs our paths, the more we will trust Him and the more our faith will grow. If you, too, have a question as to, "Should I do this or not?" ask Him. He will answer and make it very plain.

> The more God answers prayers and directs our paths, the more we will trust Him and the more our faith will grow.

WHAT AM I TO DO NOW?

Another way we hear from the Lord is through <u>God-given</u> <u>dreams</u>. After the Lord's answer was not to take the community service job, I asked the Lord as to what was to be my ministry? Just two days later, God answered this question very specifically--I had a dream!

This God-inspired dream was about a man from the Australian Outback who gave me a large bulky, white, rectangular envelope which was opened on one end. It was full of money and a lot of the bills were bulging out the top of the envelope.

Then, a little old white-haired lady came up to me on my right and said she was going to Africa as a Missionary to build a Church there. She told me she needed that money, and so I gave her the envelope with all the currency.

I met the man from Australia again who told me he was glad that the money had gone to the Missionary. I told him he would be blessed because he was giving it to God through me. I woke up and immediately recorded this experience in my Prayer Journal. Through all of this, I now knew the Lord was calling me to fund His Churches in Africa. He then immediately gave me several additional answers that this conclusion was correct:

Confirmation: Your Dream can come to pass. Maybe God has given someone a Dream said one Minister.

Confirmation: God will even speak to you in Dreams said another Preacher.

Confirmation: A third Pastor said in Haggai 1:8: God states, "Now go into the hills, bring down timber, and rebuild my house."

Look at patterns. We also hear from God after we have had several answers by taking the time and see if they relate together as a whole. Each is a piece of a puzzle. Putting them together creates the picture of what God is calling us to do. If we have an experience in which we think, "What are the odds of that happening?" be aware and pay attention because it is God's guidance and part of His answer.

> Each is a piece of a puzzle. Putting them together creates the picture of what God is calling us to do.

In Psalms 32:8, God says, "I will instruct you and teach you in the way you should go". Another version of this scripture says, "I will guide you along the best pathway for your life. I will advise you and watch over you." I heard a sermon which conveyed that God will give us guidance per this scripture. The Pastor also said that we should pray for wisdom and referred to James 1:5 which states: "If you need wisdom – if you want to know what God wants you to do – ask Him, and He will gladly tell you". The Pastor added that we are then to go the Bible, God's Word, and ask Him to speak to our hearts.

So, I did. This time, I let my Bible fall randomly open and I heard the pages turning due to a fan above me. When the pages stopped turning, I saw it was 1st Chronicles, Chapter 22 which I read. I did not understand it, so I continued to read through several chapters in the Bible, but nothing seemed right. I again let the Bible fall open, and it fell again to 1st Chronicles 22. Nothing marked those pages, so what are the odds of this happening twice? I again read this chapter, but more carefully this time seeking God's guidance.

Then the Holy Spirit quickened my understanding. I realized that though David was denied the privilege of building the Temple himself; he nevertheless could make preparations for the Temple. David collected vast amounts of materials and supplies for its construction and thus financed the building of the Temple. I believe God was telling me through this Bible story that, like David, I was to fund the building of God's Churches in Africa.

> God speaks to us when we look back at our experiences and see how they fit together.

God speaks to us when we look back at our experiences and see how they fit together. By doing this, I realized that all of these incidences correlated perfectly. Putting them together, I noted my 1st Chronicles 22:5 scripture related David was to fund Solomon's Temple (Church). Then my dream said I was to fund God's Churches; and finally, the Haggai 1:8 scripture confirmed building God's

Churches. Now I knew exactly what the Lord was calling me to do.

WHICH CHURCHES, LORD?

I now knew that the Lord's will was for me to fund the Churches. But I was totally perplexed as to which Churches. How in the world could I find this out? I knew nothing about Africa. So, I prayed and asked God to specifically identify which Churches He was calling me to support.

The next day after I prayed this prayer was Sunday, and I went to Church. The first thing I noticed was the bulletin which said, "We financially support and build Churches in Kenya Africa." An African Pastor was present with our Pastor and spoke to the Church to say thank you for financially supporting them.

When I got home from Church, I got the mail from my mailbox which I had not retrieved on Saturday. In the mail was a gift catalog for Samaritan's Purse which included building Churches in Sudan, Africa. It also provided a way to give supplies, food, clothing, and water to the African people, which I am also called to do. Again, this was a direct answer to a direct prayer. Within one day,

God had shown me which Churches and the organizations He wants me to financially support that build Churches and give assistance to the African people.

I also had another answer for supporting the African ministries from another Pastor who said that we are to be a financial blessing to the people in Uganda and Sudan. He added that the people there starve and go without shoes and clothes, and God wants you to do something about this need in Africa!

> All you have to do is pray and ask Him, and then watch for the many ways in which He answers.

You just can't get any more definite than that! God makes His will for us very clear and specific. The Lord wants us to do exactly what He has called us to do--to fulfill His plan and our purpose for being on this earth. All you have to do is pray and ask Him, and then watch for the many ways in which He answers.

GOD HONORS THE WORK OF OUR HANDS—MONEY FOR MINISTRY

Okay, God's assignment for me is to build Churches and support Missionaries and Pastors in Africa. But how am I going to raise that kind of major funding?

One way the Lord speaks to us is through <u>honoring the work of our hands and God-given ideas</u>. Psalm 90:17 states, "You would honor and establish the work of my hands." Deuteronomy 8:18 states, "Remember the Lord your God for it is He who gives you the power to produce wealth…"

About seven years ago, I had prayed for God to honor the work of my hands per this promise in Psalm 90:17 because I needed financial resources for a different ministry God had called me to. At that time, I thought the money was to be only for the Food and Clothing Ministries.

After this prayer, I was watching a show about an interior decorator who was also an artist. He was outside with a canvas set up on an easel. He took paints and poured them onto the canvas and then took a water pistol and squirted water onto the paints. This made them run and drip off the canvas.

The resulting picture was so beautiful that I decided even I, who had no artistic abilities, could do it. After all no talent was required as you just took paints, poured them out, added water, and let them flow down the canvas. It looked easy enough; no paintbrush or utensils were used.

So, I tried it. I used a large cardboard box to set the canvas in so that the spray from the water gun would not splash onto everything. I got color-matching acrylic paints and tried it. I immediately learned from this experience, if you have talent you get beautiful pictures in everything you do, but if you do not have talent, forget it! To say that mine was not okay is a vast understatement.

In total disgust, I tore down the box to throw it away. Then I noticed it. Where the paint had dripped into puddles onto the bottom of the box, it had made the most beautiful patterns. I decided then and there to try to create the art found in those puddles.

For the next two years, I kept experimenting and improving the best way to achieve the puddle effects until it was perfected. One day, I asked the Lord if this new artwork idea was from Him. I asked because at that time, I had not put two and two together to realize this new craft was the answer to the prayer for the Lord to <u>honor the work of my hands</u>.

The Lord also speaks to us through <u>miracles</u>. I prayed, "Lord, if this new craft is from you, then will you put into my paintings, an Angel, a cross, or the face of Jesus?" Just three days after this prayer, I was sitting at my sister's house creating a painting for my Mom's bedroom with Mom sitting beside me. We had just painted the walls of her room and had selected her color scheme to be aqua, cream, and gold. Using these colors, I was pouring the paints for a picture to hang on a wall in her room.

I remember, distinctly, my Mom asking me about the paints falling off at the bottom of the picture as I was creating it by flowing paints together on a canvas. I told her that did not matter; it was just part of the technique. After the large painting was finished, in about 10 minutes, I laid the painting down on paper to dry.

And there it was--my first and most beautiful Angel! She was about 10 inches tall, cream colored, had a crown, a long flowing cream colored gown and golden shoes. Her arm was raised and she was carrying a long pointer in her hand that looked like she was directing Heaven's Choir. She was also silhouetted in the gold color I had used. The location of this Angel was at the bottom boarder of the painting where the paints had been dripping off the canvas. I called it "Mom's Angel".

The Lord placed that Angel into my painting, and it can be easily proven that I did not do it. Any microscope will clearly show no drawing was done and no paint brush or tools were used to create her. It is way too intricate to try to pour paints into the shape of this Angel. It is simply a God thing -- a true miracle!

Through the years, I also have seen pictures of additional Angels, Jesus, and Mother Mary's in these paintings. One Mary looks like she is made out of gold dust, and there has been a St. Peter or the Pope as well. I believe the Lord created these Miracles so they could be sold to fund His Churches!

Also, there have been animals like a Shetland pony, cows, dogs and cats as well as various birds, fish, and dolphins. Large pictures have occurred too, such as an owl with multicolored feathers on its chest, and a bird sitting on a tree limb in a nest. Complete scenes have also been created that I did not paint. Some include ocean waves and shore pictures; land, sky and mountain scenes, and outer universe displays. God is the artist, not me; I just poured the paints. All of this was created to promote God's work and for His glory.

Do you have a God-given idea or product? If not, ask Him for one. You too may end up with divinely-inspired creations.

THE LORD'S ENCOURAGEMENT

God speaks to us when He knows we need His encouragement concerning what we are praying, hoping, and longing for will one day happen. Occasionally, time seems to stand still, take forever, and we do not believe any progress is being made. This leads to discouragement, and if it continues long enough, it can lead to hopelessness.

I was going through such a long delay that I had become discouraged concerning the funding to build and support God's Churches. One day the Holy Spirit quickened my understanding as I was reading Proverbs 22:17-19 that stated to "Listen to the words of the wise; apply your heart to my instruction." "I am teaching you today, yes you, so you will trust in the Lord."

I know God speaks to us through His Word. Taking this to heart, I paid attention to what was happening in my life that day. And there it was. My morning devotional concerned funding projects. That started the day out right!

Essentially, this message said that you may feel like you've wasted years waiting for your dream to happen. You may think it was all just your imagination and decide that it is never going to happen. But, it continued to say, that the Lord has heard every faith declaration you have made, and will supply the funding when the time is right. The Lord has also noticed all the time, energy, and commitment you've made over the years!

> God speaks to us when He knows we need His encouragement concerning what we are praying, hoping, and longing for will one day happen.

Through this message, I concluded the Lord was reassuring and encouraging me even though I was not seeing any progress in selling this God-inspired artwork to fund the Churches. I still should continue to believe and not give up.

Stay in faith and know it will happen in God's timing. This was the Word from the Lord personally to me. He reassured me that the dream He gave me was going to happen; that I would fulfill my destiny.

> Sometimes it is really hard not to give up, but then God comes through at just the right moment with a special word of loving encouragement.

Sometimes it is really hard not to give up, but then God comes through at just the right moment with a special word of loving encouragement. In other words, when the time is right, the Miracles will be displayed for the world to see and then they will sell to support God's work. It will happen. You, too, should believe for your dream. Don't give up no matter how long it takes. The Lord controls the timing. This may also be a timely word from the Lord for you, too--consider it so.

HOW DO I KNOW IT IS GOD'S TIMING?

This artwork has produced tiny figures which resemble Mother Mary, Jesus and Angels. For the last two years, I have cut these Miracles carefully out of the large paintings along with a matching Angel which I made. I glued these two items to a bookmark with "Jesus Loves You" on the back and had them laminated. Missionaries have carried these bookmarks containing the God-given Miracles to the orphans in South America, Mexico, the Bahamas, and the United States of America.

Suddenly, the laminations failed on one batch of book marks and they had to be redone. A couple of weeks later, I took in a second batch, and those also had to be redone. My heart was broken, but I never blamed the laminators because I immediately realized God had a purpose in allowing this to happen. I was praying that the Lord would help me understand what His reason was for allowing these mistakes. Was this Bookmark Ministry over?

On the way home from the laminators, I prayed for God to have my best friend call me because she was always an encourager. When I arrived at home, I noticed she had called, and I immediately called her back. She had already known about the first failed batch of laminations, but before I could tell her about the second, she said she had to tell me about the devotional that she had just read that morning. She continued that God had laid it on her heart to call because she knew it was for me. So, I just listened.

She conveyed that her devotional said in general to take courage and start a <u>new</u> life tomorrow. To put old mistakes away and start anew, and that God is giving you a fresh start. She said that she felt it is God who is stopping me from continuing with the paintings and who is ending the Bookmark Ministry. She emphasized, "It would be a mistake to continue with it." I then explained to her that the second batch had also failed, and she encouraged me that <u>God will open another door and has a new plan</u> for me.

God will open another door and has a new plan.

The Lord promptly gave me a confirmation of what my friend had just said. I turned on the television and heard a Pastor immediately convey that you are not giving up anything even though you have had a setback and suffered loss. Keep moving forward because that setback is not the end. God closes doors. He added that "It would be a mistake to continue." (The same exact words; this is not coincidence.) He related that the Lord wants you to do something new and have new things to mount on the wall and display. (Such as God's inspired pictures.) He finished by saying to not to let your circumstances discourage you. God is in control and you will accomplish your dreams.

NOW THE ISSUE IS: HOW TO DISPLAY AND SELL THE <u>MIRACLES</u>

I believe with all my heart the good Lord means that now is the time to sell His Supernatural Artwork which I call "God's Miracles". I don't say that lightly because it has been several years that I have known my purpose was to sell the art. Now is the time for me to display and showcase "God's Miracles". This is the way God has chosen to fund and further His kingdom by providing for the African Churches, Missionaries, and peoples.

God continues to bring Christian people into my life to help with His work. I walked into a Christian Writing Class, for the first time, and one of the writers there, Sue Harrington, is a Publishing Coordinator. (Sue's Author's Page on amazon.com is Susan L. Harrington and her email is <u>storiesforpublication@yahoo.com</u>). Sue offered to waive her fees and publish this book during her busy season in less than <u>one month!</u> Sue is charging me no fees and no out-of-pocket costs to publish the book! Our meeting was a <u>Divine Appointment</u> just so this book could be published immediately. God is in control of our steps for His purposes!

ADDITIONAL THOUGHTS

After you have ascertained God's answers, obey the Lord and do what He is calling you to do. Be faithful to your ministry. Finish your tasks, fulfill your responsibilities, keep your promises, and complete your commitments. Don't leave a job half undone, and don't quit when you get discouraged. Be trustworthy and dependable to what God called you to do. Then, one day, you will hear the Lord say to you as in Matthew 25:23, "Well done, my good and faithful servant."

> After you have ascertained God's answers, obey the Lord and do what He is calling you to do.

When you do good deeds, don't take the limelight and pat yourself on the back. And definitely don't take the credit away from God. Be absolutely sure the person you are helping understands that it was God who sent you to them, and especially relay that God loves and cares for them. Give God all the credit, glory, and praise that He deserves.

The Lord put you where you are for a specific purpose. He knows your address, and you need to stay and serve right where you are until God chooses to move you. The Lord wants you to use every opportunity to share your testimony with those He puts in your path. These <u>Divine Appointments</u> are specific to you and the people God sends to you. Take advantage of opportunities. Remember God loves you, and we are to love others and show God's love through our service.

> Give God all the credit, glory, and praise that He deserves.

DELIGHT YOURSELF IN THE LORD AND WATCH WHAT HAPPENS!

This is based on Psalm 37:4 which states, you are to "Delight yourself in the Lord." I wanted to share this with you because it will strengthen your relationship with the Lord as you seek His answers and presence. God loves to answer this prayer.

The question is: "How do we delight ourselves in the Lord?" It is as easy as "1, 2, 3"!

A few years ago a Pastor gave a sermon concerning how to do it. He related the following:

First, when you wake up in the morning pray that the Lord will let you see His presence throughout the day.

Secondly, proceed with your normal day, but note anytime that you see anything related to the God, Jesus, and Christianity.

Thirdly, simply praise God. Quietly, unobtrusively, privately just praise Him and thank Him for being with you, for hearing your prayer, answering your prayer, letting you know that He is with you, letting you encounter His presence, and letting you experience that He loves you.

Silently in your thoughts, tell Jesus how much you love Him. Bless Him, thank Him, and especially praise Him!

That is all there is to it, and you will be <u>amazed</u> that the Lord will honor this prayer 100% of the time every day that you pray it. He will honor this request by letting you see His presence through having you note Christian things and activities. This means you instantly become aware that God has just answered your prayer, and because of that, you feel He is walking right beside you. You then know the Lord is present with you at all times, which is so very comforting. He hears you and is answering.

Some of my experiences with the Lord after praying this prayer include: seeing a Church steeple or billboard advertising something Christian; seeing a family holding hands and saying grace at a restaurant; seeing someone reading their Bible in an airport; seeing Christian bumper stickers. Each time I saw this; I simply quietly praised and thanked Him for answering this prayer.

I have personally found God will deliver special blessings to you and maybe even provide "an Angel or two unawares" in order to honor this prayer.   I have experienced all of these while praying this specific prayer every day for 100 straight days. Below I have listed a few of my own special God-inspired answers.

Once, it was late in the day and I was going home from work when I realized that I had not experienced the Lord's presence that day, and I reminded Him of it. Just as I finished telling the Lord this, a car passed me on the right side that had a hand-written brown cardboard sign in the back window of a car that said, "Jesus Loves You!" That exact timing makes this a very special touch of God's favor. This event is different from another similar occurrence mentioned earlier.

Two other times I was in the same restaurant in Memphis, Tennessee. The first time I asked the Lord to let me see His presence while I was there during lunch and I overheard two men across the aisle talking about Romans Chapter 8 in the Bible. I got up and went over to them and related what I had just prayed and that they were God's Divine Appointment to honor this prayer.

Another time, I was at this same restaurant and again prayed this same prayer. As I was checking out, a man was talking to the lady at the cash register about the Book of Revelation, in the Bible, and that we are living in the last days before the return of Christ. (Amen!)

Once again I was driving home from work and remembered the Lord had not provided His presence through something Christian so that I could delight myself in Him by praising Him. I immediately opened my sun roof, looked up, and saw a perfect white cross in the sky from the contrails where two jets had crossed each other's paths. This to me was a supernatural event because look at the timing, and it was directly above my car!

At another time, I was in a restaurant in my home town, and remembered I had not prayed to see God's presence that morning. So, I closed my eyes and prayed. The moment I opened my eyes, I saw a cold storage food truck pass by the restaurant's front window which I was facing. The entire side of this truck was painted with Jesus and the 12 disciples sitting at the table at the Lord's Supper.

But it gets better! I was so overjoyed that the Lord had answered so quickly that I must have tightly closed my teary eyes as I was quietly thanking, praising, and thus delighting myself in Him. I say this because two ladies who had been sitting at a table close by, not understanding, actually got up and came over to my table and said to me, "Jesus Loves You!" (Wow--double answers!)

On another occasion, I had returned all the way home very late from a very long day at work and instantly realized that I had not heard from the Lord at all that day. I lamented this to the Lord because for weeks He had never failed me even once. But the Lord must have had a smile on His face as I took out a new brand of frozen pizza from the freezer. (I will never forget it.) There on the front of the box was a scripture! That was a special touch from God just for me to see His presence. How many times have you seen scriptures on pizzas?

My most favorite of all my special times with the Lord, through requesting to see His presence so I could delight myself in Him, was experienced in Toronto, Canada. I prayed this prayer on a subway heading to downtown. I got off the subway and was walking up a street when a lady approached me on the left speaking French and holding out a brochure. Since I did not speak French, I waved her off and kept walking.

Suddenly, I heard the word spoken in perfect English from her to me, "prayer". I immediately smiled and was silently praising God for answering my prayer by seeing His presence. I half-turned toward her and waved when she pointed her finger at me and said, also in perfect English, "I thought that would bring a smile to your face." Was she an Angel? Perhaps she was. The scriptures say we do "entertain Angels unawares", and how else can you explain this? I can't. Thinking back on it, how did she know what I was silently praying, and her comments fit perfectly as the answer to this prayer. Delight yourself in the Lord; it will bless you!

Now it is your turn to encounter direct answers to your prayers through this simple way to experience the Lord's presence. Then, you too will know He is with you, listening to you, and answering your prayers. What a comfort and pleasure you will derive from these experiences. Try it for yourself for 30 days and watch how God answers! I promise you will not be disappointed, and you too will experience your own special touches of God's favor that He designs just for you.

THE LORD'S BLESSING— JUST FOR YOU!

I had to add this special blessing as it was so neat the way the Lord gave it to me. As I was finishing this book, I thought about the blessing starting with "May the Lord shine His face upon you", but I could not remember all the words because it had been years since I had heard it. I thought it was in Deuteronomy and I read over it trying to find it. It was not there. Perplexed, I prayed, "Lord if you want this blessing in this book, please give it to me."

This same day, I was watching a television sermon and usually I don't watch the ads at the end of the show. But this time I did. There it was--a Pastor was saying this very blessing! What are the odds? To me it was "a God thing" and a "God blessing"! I could not find my concordance, but my sister had hers and found it in Numbers 6:24-26. So here it is-- God wanted you to have it.

"May the Lord bless you and protect you.

May the Lord's face smile upon you.

May the Lord be gracious to you.

May the Lord show you His favor.

May the Lord give you His peace."

And this is my prayer for you, too:

God bless you!

Made in the USA
Charleston, SC
14 October 2016